C o n t e n t s

Words in **bold** in the text are explained in the glossary on page 44.

Cicero

106-43 BC

'There isn't a place which has not been invaded by the greed and injustice of our fellow Romans ... It is hard to find words to say how much foreign nations hate us.'

This judgment on Rome was made by Cicero, an important writer, **orator** and politician. At that time, Julius Caesar was the ruler of the **empire**. Cicero thought that Caesar had too much power over the people and **provinces** of Rome. In many powerful speeches, he said that a **republic** was much better than an empire.

Cicero's way of writing Latin, the language of the Romans, had a great influence on its development. He was able to translate into Latin certain ideas and words which had only existed before in Greek. Latin became the language of educated people in Europe for many centuries. Eventually it formed the basis of modern languages such as Italian, English, French, Spanish and Portuguese.

Marcus Tullius Cicero, who influenced Roman politics and the Latin language.

OTHERS TO STUDY

Julius Caesar (see page 8).

Seneca the Elder (c.55 BC–AD 39)
– a Roman orator.

Tiberius Gracchus (c.163–133 BC)
– a Roman consul.

Memmius–governor of the
Roman province Bithynia.

HISTORY MAKERS

HISTORY MAKERS of the ROMAN EMPIRE

DR PENELOPE SCOTT
AND DR A. SUSAN WILLIAMS

ILLUSTRATED BY
JESSICA CURTIS

HISTORY MAKERS

First published in 1995 by
Wayland (Publishers) Ltd
61 Western Road, Hove,
East Sussex BN3 1JD,
England

Series editor: Katie Roden
Series designer: Tracy Gross
Book designer: Marilyn Clay

British Library Cataloguing in Publication Data

Williams, Susan
History Makers of the Roman Empire. –
  (History Makers Series)
  I. Title II. Scott, Penny III. Curtis,
Jessica IV. Series
937

ISBN 0-7502-1525-9

Typeset by Dorchester Typesetting Group Ltd, England
Printed and bound in Italy by Lego

Notes for teachers

History Makers uses a wide range of exciting contemporary sources – quotations, letters, sculptures, paintings and artefacts – to build up detailed and informative portraits of people who made important contributions both to their own time and to the way we live now.

This book:

- features important figures from all areas of life in the Roman Empire – science and technology, the arts, exploration and settlement, warfare and defence, food and health, slavery, law and government;

- presents contemporary reactions to changes and innovations;

- focuses on the effects of invasion and settlement on the countries within the empire;

- explores the structure of Roman society;

- emphasizes the importance of Roman achievements for modern life.

Picture acknowledgements:
Ancient Art and Architecture Collection (Ronald Sheridan) 6, 8, 10, 11, 12, 13, 14, 15, 19, 20, 21, 22, 24, 25, 27, 28, 29, 32, 39, 42; British Museum 18, 30, 31; Michael Holford Photographic 9, 16, 17, 40; Topham Picture Source 7, 23, 34, 35, 36, 37, 38, 41, 43 (both); Wayland Picture Library 26; Werner Forman Archive 33.

Cicero's writings have been read and studied for centuries. Queen Elizabeth I of England (1533–1603) had read all his work by the time she was sixteen! He wrote over 800 letters, some of which tell us about the use of **slaves** in Rome. He begged a friend:

*'Do send me two of your library slaves, to help glue pages, and tell them to bring bits of parchment for title-pieces. I say, you have bought a fine troupe of **gladiators**. I hear they fight splendidly.'*

This vase shows the clothes worn by gladiators, and the weapons that they used for fighting.

A slave called Tiro lived with Cicero's family, and was loved and treated well. Eventually Cicero gave Tiro his freedom, so that he could be 'our friend instead of our slave'.

Cicero adored his daughter Tullia. After her death, he said:

'I don't speak to a soul. In the morning I hide myself in the wood where it is wild and thick and I don't come out till evening …I fight against tears as much as I can, but as yet I am not equal to the struggle.'

DATE CHART

106 BC
Marcus Tullius Cicero is born in Arpinum, Italy.

84 BC
The poet Catullus is born.

63 BC
The future emperor Augustus is born.

63 BC
Cicero becomes a consul.

63 BC
He delivers four speeches against the Roman politician Catiline, who is plotting to overthrow the government.

58–57 BC
Cicero is exiled after executing the Catiline conspirators without a trial.

47 BC
Cicero divorces his wife after 30 years of marriage.

45 BC
His daughter Tullia dies.

44 BC
Julius Caesar is killed.

44–43 BC
Cicero composes 14 speeches attacking Mark Antony.

43 BC
Cicero is murdered by Mark Antony's soldiers.

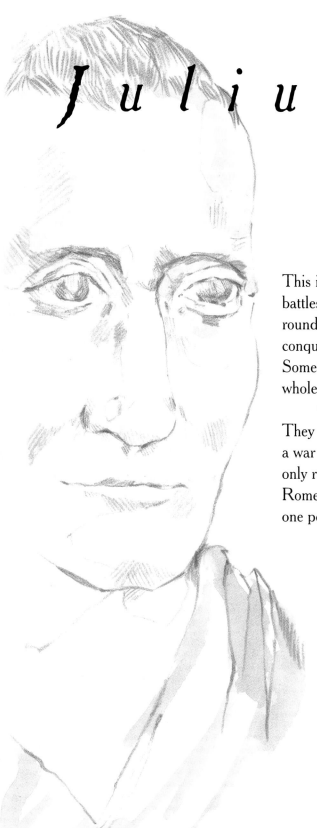

Julius Caesar

100-44 BC

'I came, I saw, I conquered.'

This is how Julius Caesar, a great army general, described his many battles. By winning some important wars, he spread the rule of Rome all round the Mediterranean Sea. For nine years, he fought a **campaign** to conquer Gaul, which we now call France. He also invaded Britain. Sometimes he was cruel to the people he conquered. He massacred whole tribes of Gauls and Germans, or sold them into slavery.

Caesar made many enemies among important Roman politicians. They ordered him to give up his army, but he refused. Instead, he fought a war against his rivals and destroyed them, then acted as if he were the only ruler of Rome. Many Romans were not pleased. They wanted Rome to stay a republic, so that power would be shared by more than one person.

This Roman medallion shows Caesar and his prisoners from Gaul.

Caesar was murdered by a group of powerful men led by Cassius and Brutus, whom he had thought of as his friends. Many people were pleased about his death, including the orator Cicero, who said:

'Our heroes accomplished most gloriously and magnificently all they could.'

Cicero even complained that he was not invited to join in with the murder. The story of Caesar's death is told in a play by William Shakespeare called *Julius Caesar*.

The remains of a Roman aqueduct in Provence, France. It was built in the first century AD.

At the time of his death, Caesar was in the middle of carrying out **reforms** in the empire. He let many people become Roman **citizens**, which meant that they had important legal rights and freedoms. He also built bridges, roads and **aqueducts**. He made the Roman calendar more accurate, and the month now called July is named after him.

9

Caesar was popular with many Romans because he organized magnificent gladiatorial games. He does not seem to have enjoyed them much, however. In a story about Augustus, who later became the first Roman emperor, it was said that:

*'As often as Augustus attended the gladiatorial games, he would take special pains to appear absorbed by the spectacle, because he wished to avoid the **odium** incurred by his relative [Caesar] who had been used, when present on such occasions, to turn away and occupy himself with reading or writing.'*

A Roman gladiator kneeling in defeat. The kneeling man is a *retarius*, or 'net man'. He had to use his net to entangle the other man, a *secutor* ('pursuer').

49 BC
Pompey orders Caesar to give up his army. Caesar refuses, wins a battle against his rivals and makes himself the only ruler of Rome.

48 BC
Caesar meets Cleopatra in Egypt. He helps her to become queen again.

47 BC
Caesar and Cleopatra probably have a son, Caesarion.

44 BC
Caesar is murdered.

41 BC
Cleopatra meets Mark Antony. They later marry and have three children.

Caesar's travels took him to Egypt, where he met Cleopatra. Cleopatra was the queen of Egypt, which later became an important part of the Roman Empire. Egypt supplied Rome with **papyrus**, which was used as writing paper, and with wild animals for shows at the **circus**.

This bust of Cleopatra is the only one
that was made while she was alive.

It is thought that Cleopatra and Caesar had a son, Caesarion.
Cleopatra went to Rome, where she lived until Caesar was killed. Not
everyone liked her. Cicero said:

*'Cleopatra. How I detest the woman. You know she lived just
across the river from me for several months.'*

OTHER ROMAN GENERALS

Pompey (106–48 BC)
– a politician who fought
against Caesar.

Agrippa (63–12 BC)
– made a consul as a reward for
his military success.

Agricola (AD 40–93)
– a governor of Britain.

11

V i r g i l

7 0 – 1 9 B C

'My master and my author, he who taught me the good style that did me honour.'

This is what Dante, a thirteenth-century Italian poet, said about Virgil. Virgil was the greatest poet of ancient Rome and his poetry has influenced writers in many countries for nearly two thousand years.

Virgil's most famous poem is an **epic** called *The Aeneid*. It tells the story of a Trojan hero called Aeneas, the son of a man and a goddess. During the Trojan war, which took place between the people of Troy and the Greeks, the life of Aeneas was believed to have been saved several times by the gods. Virgil used many sources to write this long poem, including two epics written by a Greek poet, Homer, called *The Iliad* and *The Odyssey*.

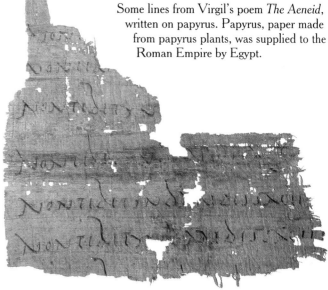

Some lines from Virgil's poem *The Aeneid*, written on papyrus. Papyrus, paper made from papyrus plants, was supplied to the Roman Empire by Egypt.

12

The real subject of the long poem was not Aeneas, but Rome and the glories of its empire. Virgil tells his readers:

'Do you, Roman, remember to rule nations with power supreme.'

Virgil died before he could finish *The Aeneid*. Although he left instructions that the poem should be burned, the emperor Augustus made two of Virgil's friends publish it. Shortly afterwards, Roman schools began to use his works as textbooks.

This mosaic from the first century BC shows a farmer ploughing a field. Virgil's poem *The Georgics* is full of advice for farmers.

Virgil lived in the country, and did not like visiting the city of Rome. His poem called *The Georgics* is about farming life. Although it is a poem, it is full of advice. In the first lines, Virgil tells his readers what the poem is about:

'What makes a cornfield smile; under what star the soil should be upturned . . . ; what care oxen need; what is the method of breeding cattle; and what is the weight of men's experience in preserving . . . bees; such is the song I now try to tell.'

OTHER ROMAN POETS

Horace (65–8 BC) – author of *The Odes*.

Catullus (c.84–c.54 BC) – author of 113 poems.

Ovid (c.43 BC–c.AD 17) – author of *The Art of Love*.

DATE CHART

70 BC
Virgil (Publius Vergilius Maro) is born.

65 BC
The poet Horace is born.

63 BC
Cicero makes speeches against Emperor Catiline.

47–45 BC
Caesar fights battles in the east of the empire, Africa and Spain.

30 BC
Virgil writes *The Georgics* and starts writing *The Aeneid*.

27 BC
Rome becomes a republic again.

25 BC
The poet Ovid begins writing *The Art of Love* (Amores).

19 BC
Virgil dies.

2 BC
Emperor Augustus is named 'Father of his Country'.

13

Livia

58 BC – AD 29

'She guarded her good name jealously.'

This is how a Roman writer described Livia, the wife of Augustus, the first Roman emperor. She was married to another man when Augustus fell in love with her. He forced her husband to divorce her, even though she was pregnant with a son, the future emperor Tiberius. Then they married and lived happily together for fifty-three years, until Augustus died. She gave him advice on how to run the empire. Through her influence, Augustus showed mercy to people who plotted against him.

Augustus's love for Livia was talked about everywhere. It was even used to explain why the poet Ovid was sent away from Rome to a town by the Black Sea, where he was cold and miserable. People said that Augustus had punished him because he had seen Livia in her bath.

A Roman wedding ceremony. Emperor Augustus was so in love with Livia that he persuaded her to divorce her first husband and marry him.

OTHER WOMEN IN IMPORTANT ROMAN FAMILIES

Terentia and Tullia – wife and daughter of Cicero.

14

A bust of Livia Drusilla, made in about 30 BC.

After the death of Augustus, the terms of his will adopted Livia into his family and gave her the special title of Augusta. This changed her name to Julia Augusta. Under Roman law, it also meant that she became the adopted daughter of Augustus.

Livia was declared a goddess many years after her death, just as Augustus had been made a god when he died. A temple was built in their honour at Vienne in France, which can be visited today.

In the Roman Empire, women took religion just as seriously as men. They believed that their future life would be arranged by the gods and spirits. A Roman poet wrote that:

'Poor women make for the circus track, where they get their heads and hands read, making sure they smack their lips to ward off the evil eye. Rich women hire fortune-tellers from the mysterious East.'

DATE CHART

186 BC
Women are allowed to choose their own tutors.

63 BC
Birth of the future emperor Augustus.

58 BC
Livia Drusilla is born.

44 BC
Caesar is murdered.

c.43 BC
Livia marries Tiberius Claudius Nero.

39 BC
Livia is divorced from Nero and marries the emperor, Augustus.

30 BC
Deaths of Antony and Cleopatra.

18 BC
A law is passed which allows a father to kill his own daughter in certain circumstances, such as adultery.

12 BC
Livia's son Tiberius is forced to divorce his wife and marry someone else.

AD 29
Livia dies.

Celsus

c.25 BC – AD 50

'A tumour grew from no apparent cause, the doctors cried out all sorts of things, but the god gave me the opposite opinion and told me to endure and foster the growth, and clearly there is no choice between listening to the doctors or the gods.'

This comes from the diary of a well-educated Roman. It shows that Roman people trusted gods more than doctors when they were ill.

Even so, many of them visited doctors. Celsus was the author of an encyclopedia which included *De Medicina*, the greatest work on medicine to have survived from Roman times. It is very long, and describes many treatments and operations. It was written in a simple style of Latin so that ordinary people could understand it. Celsus was not a doctor, but he probably treated the servants and slaves in his household.

Roman medical instruments from the first century AD. They include a box for drugs, a bleeding cup, a scalpel and a spoon.

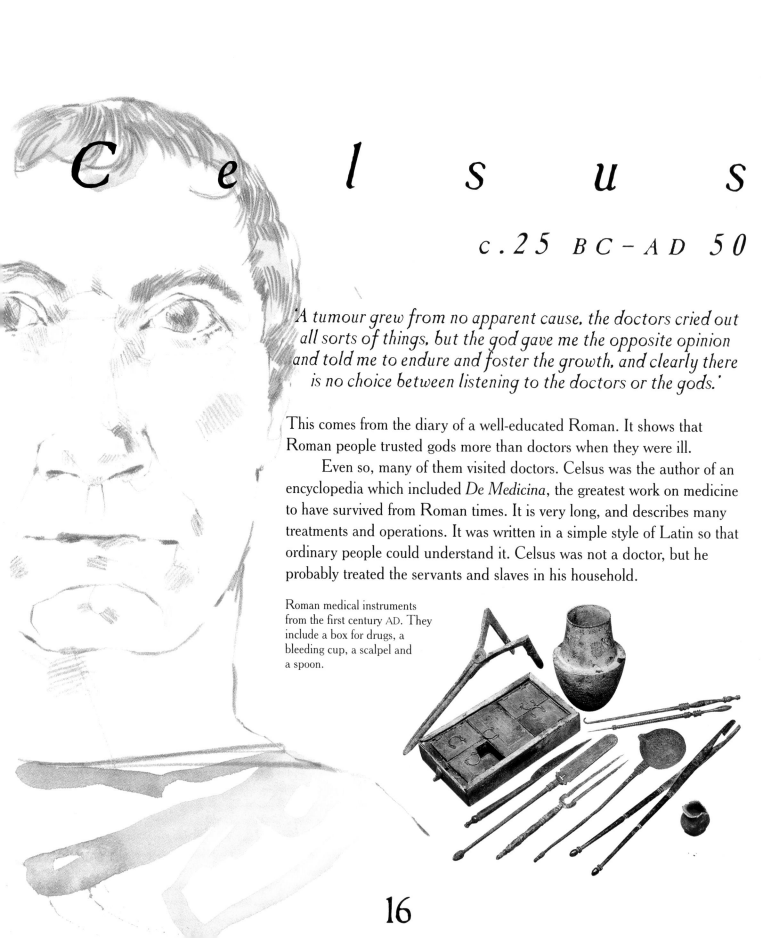

16

Bathing was believed to cure many illnesses. These Roman baths can still be visited in Bath, England.

Most of the medicines listed by Celsus were made of herbs and vegetables. A popular way of treating illness was bathing. Public baths were built all over the empire, including in Britain; it was the Roman baths that gave the English city of Bath its name. Celsus explained that:

'Now the bath is of double service: for at one time after fevers have come down, it prepares the patient for a fuller diet and stronger wine; at another time it actually takes off the fever.'

During the Middle Ages (c.1100–1500), Celsus's book had a great influence on medicine. It became the first **classical** medical work to be printed. Today, *De Medicina* gives us an important understanding of how illness was treated in Roman times.

DATE CHART

c.25 BC
Aulus Cornelius Celsus is born.

19 BC
The poet Virgil dies.

First century AD
Date of the earliest surgical instruments that have been found in modern times.

AD 9
The historian Livy completes his history of Rome.

AD 30
Celsus writes *De Medicina*.

AD 50
Celsus dies.

OTHER ROMAN SCIENTISTS

Soranus
– a doctor of the first century AD.

Pliny the Elder (AD 23–79)
– a natural historian.

17

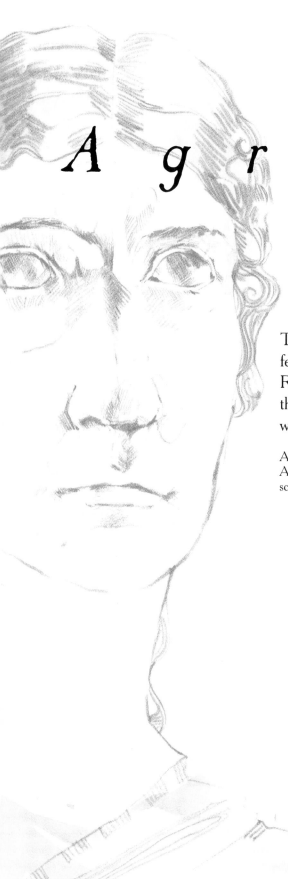

Agrippina

c.14 BC – AD 33

'She is a big-hearted woman.'

This admiration of Agrippina the Elder was written by one Roman, but felt by many. Agrippina has been called the bravest woman of ancient Rome. She accompanied her husband Germanicus, who was a general in the army, on dangerous military campaigns. This was rare for Roman women, who usually had to stay at home while the men were away fighting.

A bust of a Roman empress, probably Agrippina the Elder, by an unknown sculptor.

This carving from 25 BC originally showed two freedwomen. However, it was later re-cut to show a wife and husband holding hands.

We do not have much information about Roman women, because Roman society was organized by men. Women in rich families lived a very private life, cut off from the rest of the world.

Life was different for poor women, slaves and **freedwomen**, many of whom had to work. This meant that they took a fuller part in the world outside the home. Women even fought as gladiators. You can still see an **inscription** at a holy place near Rome, which shows that four freedwomen ran an eating-house there:

'Flacceia Lais, freedwomen of Aulus, Orbia Lais, freedwoman of Orbia, Cominia Philocaris, freedwoman of Marcus, Centuria Thais, freedwoman of Quintus, set up a kitchen for Venus, at their own cost.'

OTHER WOMEN IN ROMAN HISTORY

Agrippina the Younger (AD 15–59)
– mother of Emperor Caligula.

Octavia (?–11 BC)
– daughter of Augustus.

Cornelia (?–67 BC)
– wife of Julius Caesar.

19

Roman women married at an early age and spent their lives caring for their children and homes. It was legal for girls to marry as young as twelve, and some were engaged when they were even younger. Tullia, the daughter of the famous writer Cicero, became engaged at twelve, married at sixteen, and was a widow at twenty-two.

Agrippina was brought up like other Roman girls in wealthy families. They did not go to school like their brothers, but were taught how to read and write by their mothers and slaves. Some women spent much of their time studying and reading. The letter-writer Pliny said that his wife:

'... likes reading a lot ... She has all my books, which she reads. She has also learnt them by heart.'

Roman women were not allowed to go to school, but were taught to read and write at home. This picture of a girl reading was found in Pompeii, Italy.

When Agrippina's husband died during a campaign in the eastern part of the empire, she came back to Rome with her nine children. Large crowds of people turned out to greet them. Agrippina's return did not please the emperor Tiberius, who was jealous of her great popularity with the people.

A Roman coin showing the head of Tiberius (AD 14–37). Tiberius was jealous of Agrippina, and banished her from Rome.

Agrippina decided to stand up to Tiberius by forming a **political party**. Her aim was to win the throne for one of her sons. This made Tiberius even more angry. He invited Agrippina to dinner, but she was warned of a plot to poison her and did not eat any food. She even refused an apple that was chosen for her by Tiberius himself.

The emperor tried to destroy Agrippina. He would not let her marry again, even though she told him how lonely she was. Then he banished her and her family to an island off Naples. While she was there, she was beaten by a Roman soldier and lost an eye. Eventually she starved to death.

AD 15
Birth of her daughter, Agrippina the Younger.

AD 18–19
Agrippina accompanies Germanicus to Armenia.

AD 26
Emperor Tiberius refuses to allow her to marry again.

AD 29
Tiberius banishes her to the island of Pandataria.

AD 33
Agrippina dies of starvation.

21

A p i c i u s

1st century BC

'Suckling pig à la Frontinus: fillet, brown, and dress; put in a casserole of fish-sauce and wine, wrap in a bouquet of leeks and dill, pour off the juice when half-cooked. When cooked, remove and dry, sprinkle with pepper, and serve.'

This recipe is in a Roman cookery book. It was probably written by a man called Apicius, but we know very little about his life. All we know is that he lived in the first century BC and loved good food! His book tells us much about what the Romans ate and how they liked to cook. The recipes use wine, vinegar and oil, as well as herbs like oregano and thyme, and spices like nutmeg and ginger.

A chef carries in a suckling pig, or piglet, for a banquet in this mosaic. The meals eaten by rich Roman people were often very luxurious.

A noblewoman enjoying a meal, from the second century AD. Look at the dog waiting for scraps!

The Romans liked to add sauces to their food. They ate the meat of farm animals such as chickens, pigeons and pigs, as well as wild boar and deer, which they hunted. Fish and shellfish were also popular, and corn was used to make bread and porridge. Dessert was fresh and dried fruit, and sometimes cakes. Honey was used to sweeten food. Wine was drunk during a meal, usually mixed with water.

Roman people ate very little food early in the day, and had their main meal in the middle of the afternoon. Wealthy people ate splendid banquets from low tables, lying down on cushions and propping themselves up with their elbows. They used their hands to eat. Some clever cooks liked to disguise the dishes so that no one could tell what was in them. At one smart banquet:

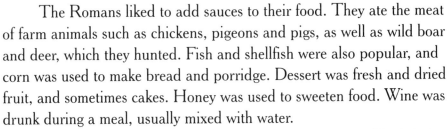

'Some very classy starters were brought in . . . on the entrée dish was a donkey of Corinthian bronze with double panniers, green olives in one and black in the other. Two dishes covered the donkey and they had the name [of the host] and their weight in silver engraved on the edges. Some little bridges supported dormice seasoned with honey and poppyseeds. There were boiling hot sausages, too, in a silver grill, and underneath were plums and pomegranate seeds.'

OTHERS TO STUDY

Trimalchio
– known as a very greedy man.

Horace (65–8 BC)
– a poet who poked fun at the greed of many Romans.

DATE CHART

100 BC
Julius Caesar is born.

First century BC
Roads are built in Italy.
Apicius is born.

82–80 BC
Sulla is made ruler of Rome.

58–57 BC
Cicero is exiled from Rome, then returns.

47–44 BC
During Caesar's reign, 150,000 poor households receive free daily corn in Rome.

Second century AD
The number of households getting free corn rises to 175,000.

S p a r t a c u s

1st century BC

'Nowadays our households contain slaves of every nationality, every creed ... Fear is the only way to keep this rubbish in check.'

Prisoners like these men were usually made into slaves.

This was the belief of a Roman historian called Tacitus. It was not true of the slave called Spartacus, who was not afraid to escape to freedom. He led a slave rebellion that defeated the Roman army in several battles in southern Italy. At one point, the slaves controlled the whole of the toe, or tip, of Italy. (It is called the toe because Italy looks like a boot when it is drawn on a map.) There were 40,000 slaves in Spartacus's army.

This mosaic from Pompeii shows wealthy people enjoying a banquet. You can see their slaves waiting on them.

The remains of the Colosseum, a huge amphitheatre in Rome, where gladiators fought. Slaves were trained to be gladiators, as their lives were considered cheap.

The Romans made many of the people they conquered into slaves. This meant that they owned them, just like pieces of property. They could buy and sell them, leave them to someone else when they died, or give them away as gifts. Sometimes slaves were stolen and then resold by the thief. If a woman slave had a child, it became the property of her master. Rich people had many slaves – men, women and children. They used them to do the hard work on their farms and estates and to do the cooking and cleaning in their homes. Slaves were often treated very badly. The Roman writer Seneca said that:

'Because smart society says that a master must be surrounded by crowds of slaves at the dinner table ... the slaves must stand absolutely silent: not a word must pass their lips – and no food either. The smallest noise is beaten back with a stick; the slaves are even beaten for letting slip a cough or a sneeze or a hiccup. The slightest sound is punished most severely. And they have to stand there all night, starving and quiet.'

OTHER SLAVES

Tiro
– Cicero's secretary.

26

Some slaves were trained in special schools to become gladiators. Roman people liked to go to the circus to watch gladiators kill each other. Thousands of cheering people would watch these shows in huge **amphitheatres**. One show in Rome lasted for 117 days, with nearly 5,000 pairs of gladiators. Sometimes the arena was sprinkled with gold dust. Some successful gladiators became very rich and famous, just like pop stars today.

The gladiator shows usually opened with wild animal fights. On one occasion, 5,000 animals – bulls, tigers, panthers and elephants – were killed. Criminals were often killed by the animals. Not everyone enjoyed these shows. One Roman asked:

'But what possible pleasure can it be to a man of culture when a puny human being is mangled by a tremendously powerful beast, or a splendid beast transfixed by a spear? The crowd took no pleasure in the elephants. Indeed, there was a kind of pity – a feeling that the huge creatures have some sort of fellowship with humans.'

A gladiator is attacked by a bear during a show at the circus.

Spartacus was being trained to be a gladiator at a special school, but he escaped with seventy fellow slaves. They were quickly joined by other slaves from all over Italy and began to form a rebellious army. The Romans were desperate to crush the rebellion, because slavery was an important part of the Roman way of life. Eventually they **crucified** Spartacus, along with many of his followers. The story of the rebellion is still remembered, however, even though slavery is now illegal in most countries. Spartacus was one of the many brave men and women throughout history who have fought against slavery.

DATE CHART

73 BC
Spartacus escapes and leads a slave rebellion.

71 BC
The Romans crush the slaves and kill Spartacus.

70 BC
Virgil is born.

68 BC
Cicero's letter-writing begins.

30 BC
Egypt becomes part of the Roman Empire and supplies animals for the circus in Rome.

AD 70–80
The Colosseum (see page 26) is built in Rome.

27

Boudicca

? – AD 61

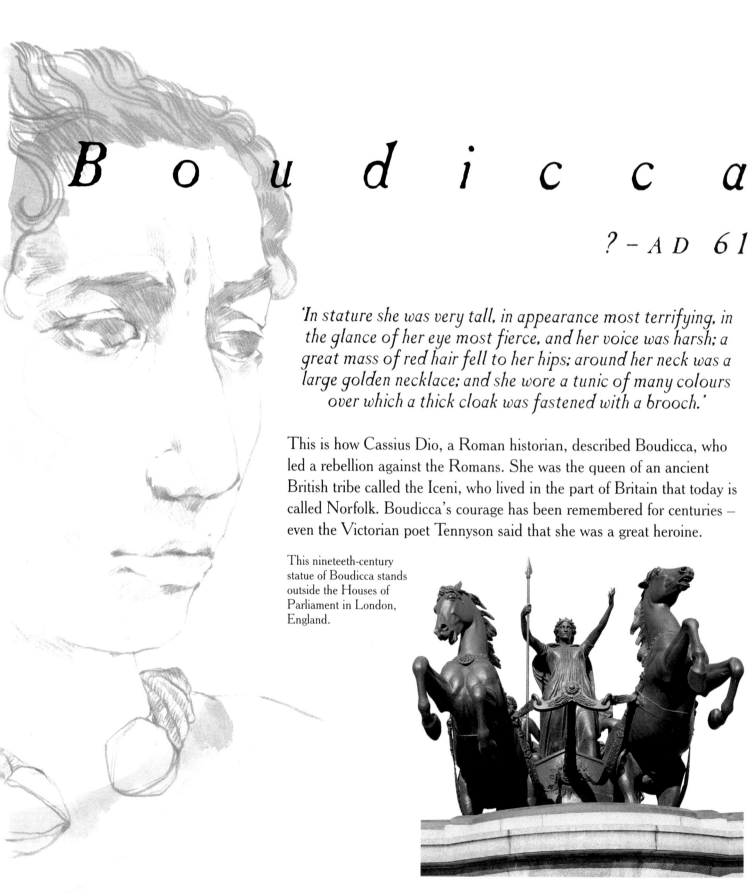

'In stature she was very tall, in appearance most terrifying, in the glance of her eye most fierce, and her voice was harsh; a great mass of red hair fell to her hips; around her neck was a large golden necklace; and she wore a tunic of many colours over which a thick cloak was fastened with a brooch.'

This is how Cassius Dio, a Roman historian, described Boudicca, who led a rebellion against the Romans. She was the queen of an ancient British tribe called the Iceni, who lived in the part of Britain that today is called Norfolk. Boudicca's courage has been remembered for centuries – even the Victorian poet Tennyson said that she was a great heroine.

This nineteeth-century statue of Boudicca stands outside the Houses of Parliament in London, England.

This Roman soldier is attacking an ancient Briton during the Roman conquest of Britain.

For a long time, the Romans tried to make the whole of Britain into a province of their empire. They seized land and made the British people into slaves, forcing them to pay taxes and to follow the Roman systems of government and religion. This made the Iceni tribe, who were proud warriors, hate them.

Boudicca, whose name means 'victory', became queen of the Iceni when her husband Prasutagus died. He had left half of his kingdom to the Roman Emperor Nero in his will, hoping that this would protect his people from the greed of the Roman governor of Britain. Sadly, his plan did not work – the Romans took all the Iceni land and gave Boudicca and her two daughters a public beating. They thought that Boudicca would be easy to crush, because she was a woman. This was a big mistake, because Boudicca had received warrior training. In the Roman army, all the soldiers were men, but many of the ancient British tribes treated men and women the same when they trained for war.

DATE CHART

55 BC
Julius Caesar's first visit to Britain.

54 BC
The Romans try to invade Britain, but fail.

AD 43
The Roman invasion of Britain begins.

29

A silver coin used by the Iceni tribe in the first century AD.

Boudicca was determined to drive the Romans away. She organized a rebellion of 80,000 British soldiers. Under her leadership, they destroyed the Roman towns of Caumulodunum (modern Colchester), which was the centre of Roman government, Londinium (London) and Verulamium (St Albans). A Roman historian said that:

'Those who stayed in Londinium because they were women, or old, or attracted to the place, were slaughtered... The same thing happened at Verulamium.'

At that time, the Roman governor was in north Wales, putting down a rebellion. As soon as he could, he marched his army to the Midlands, where he met Boudicca and her troops. His soldiers defeated the British. Boudicca killed herself with poison, rather than letting herself be killed by the Roman army.

The helmet of a Roman soldier, found in Britain.

AD 59
Emperor Nero orders the murder of his own mother.

AD 60
Boudicca becomes queen of the Iceni.

AD 61
**Revolt of the Iceni against the Romans.
Boudicca dies.**

AD 121
Romans start building Hadrian's Wall
(see pages 40–43).

AD 401
Roman troops are withdrawn from Britain to defend Italy.

This ladle was found among Roman ruins in Britain.

Her courage was not wasted, however. The Roman governor was sent home and replaced by a less cruel man. The Romans stayed in Britain for nearly four centuries. Today, there are many remains of their civilization, even an invitation to a birthday party, which was found near Hadrian's Wall. This was sent from the wife of a Roman commander to another commander's wife:

'Claudia Severa to her Lepidina greetings. On the third day before the Ides of September, sister, for the day of the celebration of my birthday, I give you a warm invitation to make sure that you come to us, to make the day more enjoyable for me by your arrival, if you come ... I shall expect you, sister. Farewell, sister, my dearest soul, as I hope to prosper, and hail.'

OTHERS TO STUDY

Cleopatra (c.69–30 BC) (see page 11).

Empress Theodora (c.AD 500–548) – co-ruler with her husband Justinian of the eastern Roman Empire.

P a u l
c. AD 3 - 67

*'When people are charged with being **Christians** I ask them face to face if this is true. If they admit it I ask them twice more, and warn them about the punishment. If they still say they are Christians I order them to be executed.'*

This was how one Roman **governor**, Pliny the Younger (see pages 36–9), treated Christians in his province. The Romans hunted down the Christians and killed them or put them in prison. They were sometimes thrown to the lions in the circus, where thousands of Romans watched them being killed for entertainment.

A lion killing a man, probably a Christian, in a Roman circus in the first century AD.

Paul was a Roman citizen who **converted** to Christianity. He persuaded many Romans to give up their religious beliefs and to become Christians like him. Eventually, Christianity became the main religion of the Roman empire and later spread to Britain.

Christians believe that there is only one god, but the Romans believed in many gods and goddesses. In order to please the gods, Roman people went to temples to leave gifts for them. They left honey, cakes, wine and coins, and wealthy people left big offerings such as ornate silver statues.

A shrine to the household gods of a home in Pompeii. This shrine stood in the atrium, or courtyard.

33

The Romans also **sacrificed** animals at **altars** in the temples, when they wanted the gods to help them. Families had altars in their homes, where they worshipped the gods and spirits who protected their households. These gods were very important, as you can see in this advice from the Roman writer Cato:

'When a new owner arrives at a farm, he should go round the farm as soon as he has paid his respects to the spirits of the house.'

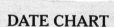

The Catacombs of Saint Calixtus in Rome, where Christians buried their dead and held secret meetings.

DATE CHART

c.AD 3
Paul is born.

AD 33
Paul converts from Judaism to Christianity.

AD 46
He goes on the first of his journeys through the empire.

AD 49
Paul's second journey.

AD 53
Paul's third journey.

AD 66–73
Revolt of the Jews against the Romans.

A carving from the third century AD, showing Paul's journey to Rome.

The Roman rulers were not pleased when Paul travelled through the empire telling people about Christianity. They were afraid that the gods would be angry. At that time, Christians were not allowed to use Roman cemeteries, so they buried their dead in underground tombs called catacombs. They also used the catacombs as secret meeting places to worship their god.

Paul was arrested and sent to Rome by ship to stand trial. On the journey, the ship was wrecked by a terrible storm. Paul survived thanks to one Roman soldier, as described in the *New Testament* in the Bible:

*'The soldiers planned to kill the prisoners to prevent any of them from swimming away and escaping. But the **centurion** wanted to spare Paul's life and kept them from carrying out their plan. He ordered those who could swim to jump overboard first and get to land. The rest were to get there on pieces of the ship. In this way everyone reached land in safety.'*

Paul was eventually executed in Rome. Before his death, he wrote about his travels and what it was like to be a Christian under Roman rule. These stories can be found in the *New Testament*.

AD 67
Paul is executed in Rome.

AD 303–5
Christians are hunted down under Emperor Diocletian.

AD 312
Start of the reign of Emperor Constantine, a Christian.

AD 313
A law is passed giving freedom of worship to Christians.

OTHERS TO STUDY

Decius (AD 201–51)
– an emperor who persecuted Christians.

Constantine (AD 280–337)
– the first Christian emperor.

35

Pliny the Younger

c. AD 62-113

'*You could hear the shrieks of women, the wailing of infants and the shouting of men; some were calling their parents, others their children or their wives, trying to recognize them by their voices ... Many asked the help of the gods, but still more imagined there were no gods left, and that the universe was plunged into eternal darkness for evermore.*'

This is how Pliny the Younger described the terror of the people of Pompeii, Italy, when their city was being destroyed. Pliny saw the **eruption** of Mount Vesuvius, a volcano near Pompeii, with his own eyes, when he was seventeen years old.

The remains of Pompeii as they are today. The city was first **excavated** in the eighteenth century.

On a hot day one summer, the volcano exploded. Molten rock and **lava** flowed quickly down to the port of Pompeii and buried it. The nearby seaside resort of Herculaneum was also buried. As far away as northern Africa and the Middle East, men and women noticed a grey dust in the air and wondered what it was. The next day, the area around Vesuvius was covered with white ash.

Two thousand people were killed, because they did not have enough time to escape. One of the victims was Pliny's uncle, Pliny the Elder, who was the leader of a fleet in the Roman navy. He breathed in poisonous gases from the lava while he was on his way to save a friend who lived at the foot of the volcano.

A man unearthed at Pompeii, lying exactly where he fell when Mount Vesuvius erupted. His body was preserved by the lava.

This loaf of bread found at Pompeii is almost 2,000 years old. You can still see the baker's name stamped into it.

Pompeii was rediscovered in the eighteenth century. Unlike other Roman cities, which have fallen into ruins over so many centuries, Pompeii was 'frozen' in time under hard ash. Excavations of the city are still going on, and give us much information about Roman life. There are **imprints** of the bodies of people and animals that were killed during the eruption. Eggshells, loaves of bread, brooches, needles and shoes have stayed just as they were nearly two thousand years ago. There are many inscriptions on the walls.

Pliny's letters give the best eyewitness account of the eruption of Vesuvius. He wrote many other interesting letters, which were published in ten books. Some of the letters describe how Pliny and his uncle, who was a scientist and historian, spent their days at home.

OTHER LETTER-WRITERS

Cicero (see pages 6–7).

Seneca (c.4 BC–AD 65) – also wrote about geography and natural history.

A Roman mosaic of sea life, found in the ruins of Pompeii.

Pliny was the governor of a Roman province, and many of the letters describe **elections** and trials at the beginning of the second century AD, when the Roman Empire was at its most powerful.

Pliny was liked by many people. He was kind to his slaves and helped his friends to get jobs. In his own town, Comum, he paid for a teacher at the school, set up a public library and started a charity for poor children. In the nineteenth century, a scholar of Pliny's letters wrote that:

'[Pliny] helped Artemidorus the philosopher to satisfy his creditors, to whom he owed a lot of money. The poet Martial received some help towards his journey home to Spain ... while an old nurse was settled comfortably on a little farm which Pliny bought for her.'

39

H a d r i a n

AD 76-138

*'From the sixth **cohort**, the **century** of Gellius Philippus built this.'*

This sentence can be found on a stone in Hadrian's Wall. It was written by Roman soldiers and tells us about this very long wall in the north of England, which can still be seen today. It was built by the Roman emperor Hadrian, to mark the northern end of the province of Roman Britain and to keep out the people of Scotland, whom he called 'the **barbarians** of the north'. It took six years to build, and is so long that it takes at least two weeks to walk from one end to the other.

Emperor Hadrian, who grew a beard to copy Greek fashion and was known as 'the little Greek'.

There is a fort on the wall called Housesteads, which has the best-preserved toilet in Roman Britain. We have been able to discover that the Roman soldiers sat on wooden seats over deep sewers. They used sponges as toilet paper, then washed them in the water in the gutter in front of them.

Hadrian was born in Spain, which was then part of the Roman Empire. His parents died when he was nine years old, and he was cared for by a relative, the emperor Trajan, who did not have any children of his own. When Trajan died, Hadrian became emperor.

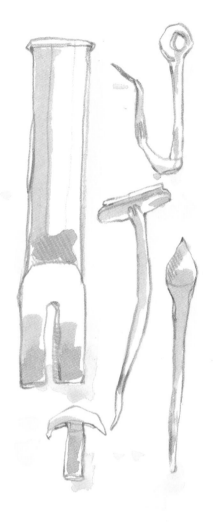

A toilet and bathroom at the Housesteads fort on Hadrian's Wall, in Northumberland, England.

OTHER ROMAN EMPERORS

Augustus (63 BC–AD 14) – the first Roman emperor.

Caligula (AD 12–41) – a very cruel emperor who went mad.

Nero (AD 37–68) – an emperor who hunted down Christians.

The remains of the magnificent library built by Hadrian in Athens, Greece.

Hadrian was very interested in the culture of classical Greece. He gave Athens, the capital of Greece, special treatment, such as a constant supply of corn and many splendid buildings. Some Romans laughed at him and called him 'the little Greek'. He copied Greek fashion by growing a beard – his enemies said that he used his beard to cover up a bad skin! A marble statue of Hadrian has been found which shows him wearing Greek clothes. Because of Hadrian, many Romans started to copy the Greek way of life.

42

For half of his reign, Hadrian travelled through the provinces of the empire. He was worried because many of the conquered people in the empire were **rebelling** against Roman rule. He took writers, map-makers, historians and engineers with him, to help him collect information about each region. He decided to strengthen the empire's **defences**. One way of doing this was to build Hadrian's Wall against the Scots. It was so well built that large parts of it still stand today.

Roman coins from the time of Hadrian. You can see a picture of Britannia on the coin on the right.

Hadrian had special coins made, each one showing a different province of the empire. The coin for Britain shows **Britannia** holding a spear and a shield, and resting a foot on the rocks.

Hadrian wanted to make the provinces of the empire feel loyal to Rome. This was necessary because the provinces gave taxes and food to Rome. One historian said:

*'Britain produces corn, cattle, gold, silver and iron and these are all **exported**, as well as leather, slaves and good hunting dogs.'*

Not every Roman thought that Britain was a useful province, however. Another person wrote that:

'There is not a scrap of silver on the island, no booty either except slaves – and I don't fancy there will be any with literary or musical talent among them.'

AD 117
Hadrian becomes emperor.

c.AD 121
The building of Hadrian's Wall begins.

AD 132–5
The Pantheon is built in Rome. Hadrian's villa is built in Tivoli.

AD 135
Coins showing different provinces are made by the mint in Rome.

AD 138
Hadrian dies.

AD 139–142
The building of the Antonine Wall in Scotland begins.

Glossary

Altar A ceremonial place for offering gifts and prayers to the gods.

Amphitheatre A circular building with seats and an open space in the middle, used for shows like gladiator fights and theatrical productions.

Aqueduct A bridge built to carry water.

Barbarians A word used to describe any people whom the Romans saw as uncivilized or vicious.

Britannia A woman used as a symbol for Britain.

Campaign A military operation or plan.

Centurion A commander in the Roman army.

Century A group of one hundred soldiers.

Christian A person who believes in Jesus Christ.

Circus An arena for games and shows.

Citizen Roman citizens had important legal rights and privileges. Many people living in the Roman Empire were not citizens.

Classical Belonging to the ancient Greek or Roman period.

Cohort A group of soldiers in the Roman army.

Consul An official appointed by the Roman state.

Convert To change your religious beliefs.

Crucify To put someone to death by nailing him or her on to a large wooden cross.

Defences Ways of protecting a place, like walls.

Election A system of voting to choose the politicians who will hold power in a country.

Empire A group of countries ruled by one nation.

Epic A long, dramatic poem.

Eruption An explosion from the earth, such as rocks and hot ash from a volcano.

Excavate/excavation To dig in the ground to find things that were buried a long time ago.

Export Sending goods to be sold in another place.

Freedwoman A former slave woman who has been freed.

Gladiator A person trained to fight with a sword or other weapons at Roman shows.

Governor A person who rules a state or town.

Imprint A mark.

Inscription Words carved on to a hard surface.

Lava The melted rock that flows from an erupting volcano.

Mint A place where money is made.

Odium Another word for hatred.

Orator A person who makes speeches.

Panniers A pair of baskets, carried by an animal.

Pantheon A temple in Rome dedicated to the gods.

Papyrus A type of ancient writing paper, first made by the ancient Egyptians from the stem of a plant.

Political party A group of politicians that wants to run a country.

Provinces The areas outside Italy that were under the rule of the Roman Empire.

Rebelling Struggling against those in power.

Reform An improvement or change.

Republic A state in which power is held by the people, instead of by just one person.

Sacrifice Killing an animal as an offering to a god.

Senate The group of people who governed Rome.

Slave Someone who is forced to work for another person, against his or her will.

Books to read

J. Badcock and G. Tingay, *The Romans and their Empire* (Stanley Thornes, 1991)

Sara C. Bisel, *The Secrets of Vesuvius* (Hodder and Stoughton, 1990)

Peter Chrisp, *Family Life In Roman Britain* (Wayland, 1994)

Peter Connolly, *The Roman Army* (Oxford University Press, 1991)

Mike Corbishley, *What do we know about the Romans?* (Simon and Schuster Young Books, 1991)

Jacqueline Dineen, *The Romans* (Heinemann Educational, 1991)

Peter Hicks, *The Romans* (Wayland, 1993)

Simon James, *Ancient Rome* (Dorling Kindersley, 1990)

Peter Mantin and Richard Pulley, *The Roman World from Republic to Empire* (Cambridge University Press, 1992)

Barry Marsden, *Roman Invaders and Settlers* (Wayland, 1992)

Michael Poulton, *Life in the Time of Augustus and the Ancient Romans* (Cherrytree Press, 1992)

Places to visit

London

Roman city wall (0171 709 0765)
There are a number of fragments, including a stretch of riverside wall in the grounds of the Tower of London.

Museum of London (0171 600 3699)
Exhibits on London in Roman times.

British Museum, London (0171 636 1555)
Roman Britain, Gallery 40; Rome: City and Empire, Gallery 70; Greek and Roman Life, Gallery 69.

Statue of Boudicca
In front of the Houses of Parliament, London.

Northern England

Hadrian's Wall
There are preserved sections of the wall running between Wallsend and Bowness. Forts along the wall include Housesteads (01434 344363) and Chesters, a cavalry fort (01434 681379).

Museum of Antiquities, University of Newcastle (0191 222 6000)
An exhibit about the history of Hadrian's Wall.

Carvoran, near Greenhead, Northumberland (01697 747485)
A Roman army museum.

High Rochester, Northumberland
The stone remains of a Roman fort.

Wales

Caerwent, Gwent
The remains of a Roman town.

Caerleon, Gwent (01633 422518)
An amphitheatre from AD 90, a bath house and fortress barracks.

Southern England

Somerset County Museum, Taunton Castle, Somerset (01823 255504)
A mosaic from a nearby Roman villa tells the *Aeneid* story of Dido and Aeneas in five scenes.

Bath, Avon (tourist office 01225 462831)
The ruins of a Roman temple and baths, and the Roman Baths Museum.

Fishbourne Palace, near Chichester, West Sussex (01243 785859)
A Roman home of the first century AD, with preserved mosaics.

Scotland

Historic Scotland (0131 244 3101)
For general information on existing Roman remains.

Antonine Wall
Stretches for 60 km from Bo'ness on the River Forth to Old Kilpatrick on the River Clyde. There were forts every 3.5 km; the best-preserved fort is at Rough Castle, 10 km west of Falkirk.

Bearsden, outside Glasgow
A bath house for soldiers.

I n d e x